KU-766-179

Religions Around the World

Sikhism

Anita Ganeri

raintree

a Capstone company — publishers for children

Raintree is an imprint of Capstone Global Library Limited, a company incorporated in England and Wales having its registered office at 264 Banbury Road, Oxford, OX2 7DY – Registered company number: 6695582

www.raintree.co.uk
myorders@raintree.co.uk

Text © Capstone Global Library Limited 2018
The moral rights of the proprietor have been asserted.

All rights reserved. No part of this publication may be reproduced in any form or by any means (including photocopying or storing it in any medium by electronic means and whether or not transiently or incidentally to some other use of this publication) without the written permission of the copyright owner, except in accordance with the provisions of the Copyright, Designs and Patents Act 1988 or under the terms of a licence issued by the Copyright Licensing Agency, Saffron House, 6–10 Kirby Street, London EC1N 8TS (www.cla.co.uk). Applications for the copyright owner's written permission should be addressed to the publisher.

Edited by Linda Staniford
Designed by Jenny Bergstrom
Picture research by Pam Mitsakos
Production by Steve Walker
Originated by Capstone Global Library
Printed and bound in India

ISBN 978 1 4747 4219 1 (hardback)
21 20 19 18 17
10 9 8 7 6 5 4 3 2 1

ISBN 978 1 474 74225 2 (paperback)
22 21 20 19 18
10 9 8 7 6 5 4 3 2 1

British Library Cataloguing in Publication Data
A full catalogue record for this book is available from the British Library.

Acknowledgements
We would like to thank the following for permission to reproduce photographs: Alamy: Ben Molyneux People, 21, David Gee, 13; Dreamstime: Kulpreet, 29; Getty Images: Richard I'Anson, 20; Newscom: akg-images/Yvan Travert, 8, 9, EPA/Raminder Pal Singh, 11, 27, Europics, 7, Hindustan Times, 23, 26, Zuma Press/Jack Kurtz, 14, Zuma Press/Manny Crisostomo, 25; Shutterstock: a katz, 5, Ajay Shrivastava, 6, Alexander Mazurkevich, 19, Anton_Ivanov, 18, AVA Bitter, cover middle, 1 middle, betto rodrigues, 28, Boris Stroujko, 4, Liudmyla Matviiets, design element, marino bocelli, 22, OlegD, 10, Sorbis, 17, Tyshchenko Photography, 15, 24; SuperStock: Eye Ubiquitous, 12; Wikimedia: Sukh, 16

We would like to thank Reverend Laurence Hillel of the London Inter Faith Centre for his invaluable help in the preparation of this book.

Every effort has been made to contact copyright holders of material reproduced in this book. Any omissions will be rectified in subsequent printings if notice is given to the publisher.

All the internet addresses (URLs) given in this book were valid at the time of going to press. However, due to the dynamic nature of the internet, some addresses may have changed, or sites may have changed or ceased to exist since publication. While the author and publisher regret any inconvenience this may cause readers, no responsibility for any such changes can be accepted by either the author or the publisher.

Contents

Some words are shown in bold, **like this.** You can find out what they mean by looking in the glossary.

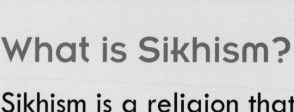

What is Sikhism?

Sikhism is a religion that began in the part of India we call the Punjab. It began about 500 years ago. Today, around 20 million people follow Sikhism.

The Golden Temple in Amritsar, India, is a very **holy** place for Sikhs.

Family life is very important for Sikh communities.

People who follow Sikhism are called Sikhs. Most Sikhs still live in the Punjab. But many Sikhs live in Britain and other countries around the world.

What do Sikhs believe?

Sikhs believe that there is one God who guides and protects them. They believe that God is everywhere and in everything. Everyone is equal before God.

The Sikh "ek onkar" symbol means "one God".

Service to the community is important to Sikhs. Many temples provide food for people.

Sikhs try to live a good life by being followers of God. They always keep God in their hearts and minds. They try to work hard, earn an honest living and help other people.

Sikhs follow the teachings of 10 **holy** men called **Gurus.** The first Guru was called Guru Nanak. Sikhs believe that God told Nanak to teach people the best way to live.

Guru Nanak was born in India in 1469 CE.

Guru Gobind Singh lived from 1675 to 1708 CE.

The 10th Guru was called Guru Gobind Singh. He did not choose a human Guru to come after him. From now on, the Sikhs' holy book (see pages 12–13) would be their guide.

Some Sikhs wear five special things as signs of their faith. They do not cut their hair (kesh) but wear a **turban** to keep their hair tidy. They also carry a small, wooden comb (kangha).

Sikhs wear a turban as a symbol of their religion. Both men and women may wear a turban.

Sikhs also wear cotton shorts (kachera) and carry a small dagger (kirpan). They wear a bracelet (kara), made from steel. These five things are known as the five Ks.

The kara reminds Sikhs to follow the **Guru's** teachings.

The Sikh holy book

The **holy** book of the Sikhs is called the **Guru** Granth Sahib. It is a collection of **hymns** and prayers. These were written by the Sikh Gurus, as well as other holy men.

The Guru Granth Sahib is written in the Punjabi language.

Sikhs try to read part of the Guru Granth Sahib every day.

Sikhs believe that the Guru Granth Sahib is the word of God. They believe that God is speaking to them through the Guru Granth Sahib. This holy book is a guide for their lives.

The **Guru** Granth Sahib is so important that it is treated like a human Guru. In a **gurdwara** (see page 16), the book is placed on a special throne in front of the worshippers.

To show **respect**, Sikhs never turn their backs on the Guru Granth Sahib.

The fan is waved over the Guru Granth Sahib as a sign of respect.

A Sikh called a **granthi** reads from the Guru Granth Sahib. He waves a fan over the book. This is the sort of fan that was waved over the Gurus to protect them from the sun.

How do Sikhs worship?

Sikhs worship at home. A Sikh family says its prayers every day. Sikhs also go to worship in a **gurdwara**. A gurdwara is a building where the **Guru** Granth Sahib is kept.

This Sikh gurdwara is in London.

When Sikhs go into the gurdwara, they take off their shoes and cover their heads. This is to show **respect**. Then they sit down on the floor, facing the Guru Granth Sahib.

There is always a light on in a gurdwara, to show that anyone can go in at any time.

At a service in a **gurdwara,** there are readings from the **Guru** Granth Sahib. There are talks about what the readings mean. People also sing **hymns** and say prayers.

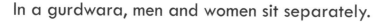

In a gurdwara, men and women sit separately.

Vegetarian food is served in the **langar** hall after the service.

After the service, everyone shares
a meal. People who are not Sikhs
are welcome. Eating together like
this was begun by Guru Nanak. He
wanted to show that everyone is
equal before God.

Saying prayers is very important for Sikhs. They believe that it is a way of spending time in God's company. They pray to God as a caring friend.

When praying, Sikhs try not to think about anything else so that they can concentrate on God.

Sikhs can pray anywhere. The words of the main prayers were written by the Gurus.

There are **set** prayers to say every day, in the morning, evening and at bedtime. These come from the **Guru** Granth Sahib. Sikhs can also say their own personal prayers.

Family times

To find a name for a Sikh baby, the **granthi** opens the **Guru** Granth Sahib and reads out a word. The parents choose a name that begins with the first letter of this word.

The baby's name also includes Singh (Lion) if it is a boy or Kaur (Princess) if it is a girl.

A turban is made of a very long piece of cloth. It takes a lot of practice to tie it correctly.

When a Sikh boy is between 10–14 years old, a special ceremony takes place in the **gurdwara**. The granthi, the boy's father or uncle helps to tie the boy's first **turban**.

The couple walk around the Guru Granth Sahib four times as they make their promises to each other.

A Sikh wedding takes place in front of the **Guru** Granth Sahib. The bride holds the end of the bridegroom's scarf to show that they are being joined as husband and wife.

Sikhs say the bedtime prayer at a funeral.

When a Sikh dies, people read from the Guru Granth Sahib. This helps to comfort the **mourners**. They also say the bedtime prayer. It reminds them that death is like a long sleep.

Sikh festivals

The most important Sikh festivals remember the lives of the **Gurus**. Sikhs celebrate Guru Nanak's birthday in November. There are **processions** in the streets in India.

A man plays a horn called a narsinga in a procession to celebrate Guru Nanak's birthday.

Reading the Guru Granth Sahib without stopping is called the Akhand Paath. It is done at other special times such as births and weddings.

During the festival, the Guru Granth Sahib is read from beginning to end without stopping. This takes about 48 hours. A team of readers takes turns to read for 2–3 hours at a time.

The festival of Vaisakhi is celebrated in April. It remembers the time when **Guru** Gobind Singh began the **Khalsa**. People drink **amrit** and promise to follow the Gurus' teachings.

Sikhs take part in colourful **processions** at the festival of Vaisakhi.

Special lamps called diyas are lit at Divali.

Divali takes place in October or November. Sikhs remember the time when Guru Har Gobind was freed from prison. People lit lamps in their houses to welcome him home.

Glossary

amrit drink made of water and sugar that is drunk at Sikh festivals

granthi a Sikh who reads from the Guru Granth Sahib, the Sikh holy book, at the temple

gurdwara a Sikh temple

Guru a Sikh holy man

holy sacred, dedicated to God

hymn song praising God

Khalsa all the members of the Sikh religion

langar kitchen in a gurdwara where food is served to all

mourner person who is very sad and missing someone who has died

procession group of people moving in an orderly way, as part of a ceremony

respect feeling of admiration or high regard

set fixed, established or provided

turban long scarf worn wrapped around the head

vegetarian a person who does not eat meat

Find out more

Books

Celebrating Sikh Festivals (Celebration Days), Nick Hunter
(Raintree, 2015)

Sikhism (Your Faith), Harriet Brundle (Booklife, 2016)

We are Sikhs (My Religion and Me), Philip Blake
(Franklin Watts, 2015)

Websites

www.bbc.co.uk/schools/religion/Sikhism/
Find out more about Sikhism with this fact-packed website.

www.primaryhomeworkhelp.co.uk/religion/sikhism.htm
Lots of information about Sikhism to help you with
homework projects.

Index